BAD
JOKES

BAD BOYS' JOKES

JOKES

Jokes you wouldn't tell the woman in your life . . .

B.S. DUCK

MICHAEL O'MARA BOOKS LIMITED

First published in Great Britain in 1997 by
Michael O'Mara Books Limited
9 Lion Yard
Tremadoc Road
London SW4 7NQ

A CIP catalogue record for this book is available from the
British Library

ISBN 1-85479-285-7

3 5 7 9 10 8 6 4

Designed by K DESIGN, Winscombe, Somerset
Printed and bound by Cox and Wyman, Reading

INTRODUCTION

Here is the cream of male jokes by the 'bad boys' I work with, do business with and drink with. Of the many hundreds of jokes I have been sent over the Internet, heard at the bar with a pint of best bitter in one hand and a pen in the other, I have only selected those my girlfriend told me were unprintable. I knew that if on the third time of reading she still found them offensive and I still found them hilarious – they had to go in.

Of the many people who contributed to this book I would like to extend my thanks to Roddy, Hendo, Donut, Mark, Bill and Justin whose combined talents have kept me out of the psychiatrist's chair and thus saved me considerable expense.

A 36-year-old single woman living at home was pleasing herself with an electrical device. Her mother walked into her room and, seeing what was going on, asked, 'What the hell are you doing?'

The woman replied, 'Mum, I'm 36 years old, I'm never going to get married and this is like a husband to me. Now leave me alone.'

The next day her father walks in on her and asks the same question, getting the same response.

About a week later, the wife walks in on her husband. He has a beer in one hand and the electrical device in his ass pleasing himself. The wife shouts, 'What the hell are you doing?'

He replies, 'Relax, I'm just having a beer with my son-in-law.'

Pinocchio was receiving complaints from his girl-friend about consummating their passions. 'Every time we make love,' she said, 'I get splinters.'

So he goes back to his maker, Gipetto the carpenter, to ask for advice.

'Sandpaper, my boy, that's what you need,' was the carpenter's response.

A couple of weeks later the carpenter saw Pinocchio again.

'How are you getting on with the girls now?' he asked.

'Who needs girls?' replied Pinocchio.

There was this typical blonde. She has long, blonde hair, blue eyes, rosebud lips, and she was sick of dumb blonde jokes. One day she decides to get a makeover, so she cuts and dyes her hair. She also goes out and buys a new convertible. She's driving down a country road and comes across a herd of sheep. She stops and calls the shepherd over.

'That's a nice flock of sheep,' she says.

'Well, thank you,' says the shepherd.

'Tell you what, I have a proposition for you,' says the woman.

'Okay,' says the shepherd.

'If I can guess the exact number of sheep in your flock, can I take one home?' asks the woman.

'Sure,' the shepherd agrees. So the girl sits up and looks at the herd for a second and then says, '382.'

'Wow!' says the shepherd. 'That's exactly right. Go ahead and pick out the sheep you want to take home.'

So the woman goes and picks one out and puts it in her car.

'Okay, now I have a proposition for you,' says the shepherd.

'What is it?' queries the woman.

'If I can guess the real colour of your hair, can I have my dog back?'

A boy walks into a whorehouse, dragging a dead, squashed frog behind him on a leash. He walks up to the Madam and says, 'I want a whore with herpes.'

'Why don't you run along, little boy,' the Madam says.

The boy plops $20 down on the table and says again, 'I want a whore with herpes!'

The Madam replies, 'All my girls are clean. I don't have any with herpes.'

The boy plops down $50 more and screams, 'I WANT A WHORE WITH HERPES!!'

'OK, OK,' the madam replies, 'this one will take care of you,' and points to a young lady on the stairs.

The lady takes him by the hand and they go upstairs, the boy still dragging the poor dead squashed frog behind him. After some time he comes back down the stairs still dragging the frog. As he is leaving, the Madam stops him and says, 'So tell me, kid, how come you wanted a whore with herpes?'

The boy replies, 'When I get home, I'm gonna have a babysitter. And I'm going to fuck the baby-sitter. Then my Dad's gonna come back and drive the babysitter home. And he's gonna fuck the babysitter. Then when he gets back he's gonna fuck my Mum. Then tomorrow, the postman's gonna come and my Mum is gonna fuck him . . . AND THAT'S THE SON OF A BITCH WHO STEPPED ON MY FROG!'

Bob complained to his friend, 'My elbow really hurts. I guess I should see a doctor.'

His friend said, 'Don't do that! There's a computer at the drug store that can diagnose anything, quicker and cheaper than a doctor. Simply put in a sample of your urine and the computer will diagnose your problem and tell you what you can do about it. It only costs five dollars.' Bob figured he had nothing to lose, so he filled a jar with a urine sample and went to the drug store. Finding the computer, he poured in the sample and deposited the $5.00. The computer started making some noises and various lights started flashing. After a brief pause out popped a small slip of paper on which was printed:

You have tennis elbow
Soak your arm in warm water
Avoid heavy labour
It will be better in two weeks.

Late that evening while thinking how amazing this new technology was and how it would change medical science forever, he began to wonder if this machine could be fooled. He decided to give it a try. He mixed together some tap water, a stool sample from his dog and urine samples from his wife and daughter. To top it off, he masturbated into the concoction. He went back to the drug store, located the machine, poured in the sample and deposited the $5.00. The machine again made the usual noise and printed out the following analysis:

Your tap water is too hard
Get a water softener
Your dog has worms
Give him vitamins
Your daughter's on drugs
Put her in rehab
Your wife's pregnant
It ain't yours . . . get a lawyer
And if you don't stop jerking off
Your tennis elbow will never get better.

A little boy from Scotland had gone to Rome on holiday with his family hoping to see the Pope. A couple of days after they'd arrived, the Pope was doing a tour of the city in his Popemobile. The little lad was a bit worried that the Pope wouldn't be able to pick him out in the crowd, so his Mum said, 'Don't worry, the Pope is a footy fan, so wear your Celtic shirt and he's bound to pick you out and talk to you.' So they're in the crowd, but the Popemobile drives past them, and stops a bit further down the street where John Paul gets out and speaks to a little boy in a Rangers shirt. The lad is distraught and starts crying. His Mum says, 'Don't worry, the Pope's driving around tomorrow as well, so we'll get you a Rangers shirt and then he's bound to stop and see you.' The next day arrives, and the boy's got on his new Rangers shirt. The Popemobile stops right by him, John Paul gets out, bends down and says to the lad, 'I thought I told you little bastard to f**k off yesterday?'

One day, a guy was riding through North Carolina and he saw a sign that said: VASELINE-POWERED CAR FOR SALE. He thought this was pretty odd, and he had plenty of time to screw around, so he decided to follow the signs to look at the Vaseline-powered car. He drove for about five miles and finally came upon a sign that pointed up a driveway, which led back into some woods. He pulled in and drove about half a mile and came upon a house. It looked deserted so he blew the horn. He waited for about a minute before an old man came out. He rolled his window down and called out to him, 'Hey! Is it true that you have a Vaseline-powered car for sale?'

The old man assured him he did and the guy asked him if he could see it. They walked back behind the house to an old barn. The old man opened the barn door and there was a car sitting under an old dirty blanket. The old man pulled the blanket off the car and under it was a shiny red Corvette.

'1969, 369 cubic inch, 400 horsepower, 4-speed transmission,' the old man said. The guy asked him if it was true that the car ran on Vaseline. And the old man went to the Vaseline tank and stuck his hand inside. When he pulled it out it was covered with Vaseline.

'Care to drive it?' he asked. As the guy snapped on his seat belt the old man said, 'Don't go too fast. Vaseline has more pick-up than regular gas. And it's low on Vaseline, too, so don't go too far.'

This guy turned the key and the car fired up and sounded like the space shuttle, then it settled down like a purring tiger. He found first gear and eased out of the barn. He turned onto the drive and hit second gear at 45mph. Third at 70 and into fourth at 95. The car felt wonderful! 110mph and so smooth! And the pick-up was unbelievable! He had covered five miles in under three minutes and all of a sudden the car shut off. He coasted to a stop and got out. To his annoyance, he found he was out of Vaseline. He started to walk.

A family had just finished supper. There was Dad, Mum and two daughters, one home from college, the other in high school. Dad was telling Mum how good supper was and Mum said that since she had cooked such a fine meal, she shouldn't have to wash the dishes. The oldest girl said that she couldn't do the dishes because she had a date and the other said she had homework to do. Dad said that he was the man of the house and he'd be damned if he did the dishes.

They argued for a few minutes and then Dad told everybody to shut up. He said what they should do is go in the living room, sit down, and the first person to say anything would have to do the dishes. They agreed and moved to the living room. They sat down and stared at each other, not speaking a word. Silence filled the room.

There was a knock at the door. A few moments later, another knock. The man at the door saw the family through the window. He knocked again but nobody answered. He walked in. 'Hey, I knocked on your door but nobody said . . . food! Do you mind if I have some?'

Nobody said anything. So he went to the table and started eating. He looked in the fridge and found some beer and asked if he could have some. Nobody said anything. He drank three or four beers and got a little buzz. He walked into the living room and asked Dad if he minded if he had sex with his oldest daughter. Nobody said anything. He took the girl to her bedroom and had sex with her. Later, he was back at the supper table drinking more beer. He walked back into the living room and asked Dad if he could have sex with his youngest daughter. Nobody said anything. He took her into her bedroom and had sex with her, too. Later, sitting at the table, after more beer, Mum started to look pretty good. He walked in and asked Dad if he minded if he had sex with his wife. Nobody said anything. So he took Mum into the bedroom and had sex with her.

When he was through he walked into the living room and stood in front of Dad. 'Hey, do you have any Vaseline?' he asked Dad. And Dad said, 'I'll wash the damn dishes.'

A husband and his beautiful wife were out enjoying a round of golf, and about to tee off on the third hole which was lined with magnificent and expensive homes. The wife hit her shot and the ball began to slice. Her shot headed directly towards the large plate glass window of a house at the edge of the course. Much to their surprise, the ball smashed through the window and shattered it. They felt compelled to see the extent of the damage but when they peeked through the broken window, they could see no one. The husband called out but there was no answer. Upon further investigation, they saw a gentleman sitting on the couch with a turban on his head. The wife said, 'Do you live here?'

'No, someone just hit a ball through the window, knocked over the vase you see there and freed me from that little bottle. I am so grateful,' he answered.

The wife said, 'Are you a genie?'

'Oh, why, yes I am. In fact, I am *so* grateful I will grant you two wishes. The third I will keep for myself,' the genie replied.

The husband and wife agreed on two wishes: one was for a scratch handicap for the husband, to which

the wife readily agreed. The other was for an income of £1,000,000 per year forever.

The genie nodded and said, 'Done!' The genie now said, 'For my wish, I would like to have my way with your very lovely wife. I have not been with a woman for many years, and after all, I have made you a scratch golfer and a millionaire.' The husband and wife agreed.

After the genie and wife were finished having sex, the genie asked the wife, 'How long have you been married?' To which she responded, 'Three years.' The genie then asked, 'How old is your husband?' To which she answered, 'Thirty-one.' The genie then asked, 'How long has he believed in this genie stuff?'

Birds of the world are symbols for different things . . .

1. What bird represents the USA?
The Eagle

2. What bird represents LOVE?
The Dove

3. What bird represents
TRUE LOVE?
The Swallow

There was a farmer who raised watermelons. He was doing pretty well but he was disturbed by some local kids who would sneak into his watermelon patch at night and eat his watermelons. After some careful thought he comes up with a clever idea that he thinks will scare the kids away for sure. So he makes up a sign and posts it in the field.

The next day the kids show up and they see this sign, which says: WARNING, ONE OF THE WATERMELONS IN THIS FIELD HAS BEEN INJECTED WITH CYANIDE. So the kids run off and make up their own sign, which they post next to the sign that the farmer made. The farmer shows up the next day to look over his field. He notices that no watermelons are missing but he notices a new sign next to his. He drives over to the sign and takes a look. It says, 'Now there are two.'

A Yank, a German and a Japanese are playing golf and bragging about their country's technologies. A phone rings and the Yank puts his thumb in his ear and pinky to his mouth and starts talking. The other two ask him how he did that.

'American technology. I have a chip in my thumb and finger.'

Three holes later and another phone rings. The German just starts talking. The other two ask him how he did that.

'German technology. I have computer chips in my tooth and ear.'

Three holes later and the Japanese goes behind a bush, drops his pants and bends over, like he's going to take a dump. The other two ask him what the hell he thinks he's doing.

'I'm waiting for a fax.'

A newly-wedded couple book into their honeymoon suite in a quaint English farm. They immediately bolt the door and are not seen for a fortnight. The farmer gets a little worried and calls up to their window.

'Are you two alright up there?' he asks.

'Fine, thank you,' comes the reply.

'Well, I haven't seen you come out of your room for ages and I wondered what you were living on,' he said.

'We're living on the fruits of love,' they replied.

'Oh, I see,' said the farmer. 'In that case, can you stop throwing the skins out of the window 'cos they're choking me chickens!'

A guy is having marital problems. He and the wife are not communicating at all and he's lonely, so he goes to a pet shop thinking a pet might help. The shop he went into specializes in parrots. As he wanders down the rows of parrots he notices one with no feet. Surprised, he mutters, 'I wonder how he hangs onto the perch?'

The parrot says, 'With my prick, you dummy.'

The guy is startled and says, 'You certainly talk well for a parrot.' The parrot says, 'Of course, I'm a very well-educated parrot. I can discuss politics, sports, religion, almost any subject you wish.'

The guy says, 'You sound like just what I was looking for.'

The parrot says, 'There's not much of a market for maimed parrots. If you offer the proprietor ten pounds for me I bet he'll sell me.'

The guy buys the parrot and for three months things went well. When he comes home from work the parrot tells him Major said this, Arsenal won, the Pope did so and so.

One day the guy comes home from work and the parrot waves a wing at him and says, 'Come in and shut the door.'

The guy says, 'What's up?' The parrot says, 'I

don't know how to tell you this, but the postman came today. Your wife answered the door in her negligee and he kissed her right on the lips.'

The guy says, 'Oh, a momentary flight of passion.'

The parrot says, 'Then he fondled her breasts.'

The guy says, 'He did?'

The parrot says, 'Then he pulled her negligee down and started sucking on her breasts.'

The guy says, 'My God, what happened next?'

The parrot says, 'I don't know. I got a hard on and fell off my perch.'

A child comes home from school and finds his Mum and Dad making love with Mum on top, bouncing up and down. He says, 'Mum, what are you doing?'

'I'm flattening Dad's tummy,' replies the mother.

'Don't bother,' says the child, 'because when you go out to work the maid will just come in as usual and blow it back up again.'

The hillbilly man and his new wife were on their honeymoon. The husband jumps into bed to wait for her to get herself ready. The wife comes out of the bathroom in a sexy negligee and says, 'Honey, I have something to tell you. I am a virgin.'

The man grabs his clothes and rushes out of the house yelling at the top of his lungs, straight towards his father's house. When he gets there his father asks, 'Son, what are you doing here? You're supposed to be on your honeymoon.' The son replied, 'Dad, my new wife told me a big secret. She's a virgin.'

'Damn, son. You did the right thing by leaving. If she wasn't good enough for her family, she sure as hell isn't good enough for ours.'

A man was standing on the hard shoulder trying to hitch a lift. A truck pulled up. The hitch-hiker opened the door and hopped in. He turned and thanked the driver, looked behind him and noticed a monkey in the back. He thought nothing of it. After driving about a mile and a half the driver pulls out a stick and whacks the monkey in the head. The monkey jumps on his lap and starts sucking his dick. The hitchhiker can't believe his eyes but says nothing. Again, another mile and a half go by, the driver pulls out a stick and whacks the monkey on the head. The monkey jumps on his lap and starts sucking his dick. The hitchhiker still can't believe his eyes. The driver turns to the hitchhiker and says, 'You want to try?'

The hitchhiker says, 'OK, but don't hit me too hard.'

God wants to go on vacation. The angels tell him, 'Well, how about Pluto?'

God said, 'Well no. Last time I went to Pluto I went skiing and broke my leg.'

So then the angels said, 'Well, how about Mercury?'

God said, 'No, last time I went to Mercury I got really badly sunburnt.'

The angels said, 'Well, how about Earth?'

God said, 'No way! The last time I went to Earth I knocked up some Jewish broad and they haven't stopped talking about it since!'

A friend of a friend was speeding and had got enough tickets before, that if she got another, she'd lose her licence. Of course, she got pulled over and was frantically trying to figure out how to talk her way out of the ticket. When the cop came up to the car she rolled down the window and said, 'Officer, you didn't pull me over because you wanted to ask me to the policeman's ball, did you?'

The cop replied, 'Cops don't have balls.'

Then there was this pause and without saying anything, the cop turned around and walked back to his car and drove away.

A very attractive girl is getting married to this extremely rich old geezer expecting him to croak soon and to inherit all his money. She does not expect anything sexual to be asked of her. After the wedding they retire to the bridal suite where she slips into something comfortable and goes straight to bed. The old geezer spends ages in the bathroom. Finally he comes out with big wads of cotton wool stuck in both his ears, a clothes peg on his nose and a condom on his todger. The girl is stunned.

'What's all that for?' she exclaims.

The old geezer replies, 'If there are two things I can't stand, it is screaming women and the smell of burning rubber!'

How do you get
a nun pregnant?

Dress her up as an altar boy.

A Frenchman and an Irish bloke were in the woods hunting one day when a beautiful girl, totally naked, turns right across their path. 'Ooh la la, oui, oui, wouldn't I like to eat that!' says the Frenchman, smacking his lips. So Paddy shot her.

Three British institutions were commissioned by the Government to discover why the penis is shaped as it is. Oxford University spent £500 over two years. They concluded that the head is wider than the shaft so that it fits better to prevent leakage and increase chances of fertilization. Cambridge spent three years and £750 to show that the head is wider because it maximizes the number of nerve endings stimulated during intercourse; this leads to increased sensitivity and a better chance of impregnation. The Open University spent £2.50 on a copy of *Playboy* and ten minutes in the staff toilet to discover that the penis widens at the tip to prevent the hand from slipping off the end.

Two guys were having a drink in a pub.

'I feel so embarrassed,' said the first. 'I walked into the library to borrow a book and was so distracted by the librarian's breasts that I asked her whether she had Dickens' *A Sale of Two Titties*.

'Don't worry,' said his mate. 'Slips of the tongue happen all the time. Only this morning at breakfast I wanted to ask my wife to pass the margarine, instead of which I said, "You bloody bitch, you ruined my life."'

A guy died with a huge hard on and the funeral director didn't know what to do. He tied it to his leg, but that only made his leg stick out of the coffin. He strapped it to his belly, but it only made him sit up, so he rang the dead guy's wife and asked her.

'Cut it off and stick it up his arse.'

The funeral director did as instructed. The day of the funeral comes and all the mourners are filing past the open coffin and the corpse has a very pained look on his face. His wife leans in and says, 'See, you bastard, I told you it hurts!'

A condom company wanted to know how many condoms to put into a box, so they did a survey. They asked an American how many condoms there should be in a box. He said seven. When asked why he said Monday, Tuesday, Wednesday, etc.

Then they asked a Frenchman how many condoms there should be. He answered nine. When asked why he said Monday, Tuesday, Wednesday, Thursday, Friday, two on Saturday and two on Sunday.

And finally the company asked an Englishman how many there should be in a box. He said twelve. The company was astonished and asked why. The English guy said January, February, March . . .

A man goes into a bar together with a cat on his shoulder and an ostrich. The bartender asks him what he wants. The guy doesn't have the chance to say anything when the cat says, 'I'll have a double whisky but I won't pay for it.' After a while the bartender comes back and asks if further drinks are desired.

'I'll have a double whisky but I won't pay for it,' says the cat again.

The guy looks very pissed off. The same scenario repeats itself a couple of times and the guy is steaming with fury. The bartender then asks him what's wrong.

The guy says, 'I found a genie in a lamp who gave me a free wish. I wished for a tall bird with a tight pussy and this is what I got.'

A man catching the last train home at night accidentally fell asleep and missed his stop. Upon waking at the end of the line in the small hours he tried to get a taxi home. He only had £5 with him and the only cabbie there told him the fare would be £10. The man offered to pay the difference when he got home but the taxi driver wasn't having it. The man spent the night sleeping rough and planning his revenge.

The next week the man caught the last train and deliberately stayed on until the last stop. The same taxi was parked there, third in the queue. The man approached the first taxi and asked how much a fare to his home would be.

'Ten pounds,' was the reply.

The man said that he only had £5 on him but he'd give the driver a blow-job as well. The taxi driver swore at him and told him to leave him alone.

The man then went to the second taxi and did the same. He got the same response.

He then went to the third taxi, the one that was there last time. Again he asked how much the fare home would be.

'Ten pounds,' was the reply.

'Okay,' said the man and got in.

As they pulled out past the first two taxis the man smiled and winked at the two drivers.

Man walks into a bar, sits down and asks the barman, 'Is it OK if I tell an Irish joke?'

Barman says, 'You see that huge fuck-off prop-forward over there with the broken nose? He's Irish. And you see the bloke next to him with the tattoos? He is from Ireland too.' The bloke hesitates and the barman points down the bar.

'You see that big bastard wrestler down there? He is Irish and that geezer he's chatting to, the one carrying the claw hammer and electric drill, he is also Irish – and by the way I am Irish as well.' The man at the bar falls silent for a while.

'Bloody hell, I'd better not tell the joke then. It'd take too fucking long to explain it to all of you.'

A cowboy is riding across the plains of the old west when he is captured by Indians. The tribe puts him on trial for crimes against the Indian Nation and he is found guilty.

'You have been sentenced to death,' said the Chief, 'but, as is our custom, you have three wishes to make as your last requests.'

The cowboy thought for a minute and said, 'Well, for my first wish, I'll need my horse.'

'Give him his horse,' said the Chief.

The cowboy whispered something into the horse's ear and the horse took off like a shot across the prairie. Twenty minutes later, the horse returned with a beautiful blonde woman on its back. The cowboy looked at her, shrugged his shoulders and helped the young lady off the horse. He then took her into the woods and had his way with her.

'Second wish,' said the Chief.

'I'll need my horse again,' said the cowboy.

'Give him his horse,' said the Chief.

Once again, the cowboy whispered into the horse's ear, and once again the horse rode off over the prairie. Thirty minutes later, the horse returned with a beautiful redhead on its back. The cowboy looked up, shrugged, helped the young lady off the horse and went into the woods, for the same reason as before.

'This is your last wish,' said the Chief. 'Make it a good one.'

'I'll need my horse again.'

'Give him his horse,' said the Chief.

The cowboy grabbed each side of the horse's head and put his face right up to the horse's.

'I SAID POSSE!!!'

A boy was crossing a road one day when a frog called out to him and said, 'If you kiss me, I'll turn into a beautiful princess.' He bent over, picked up the frog and put it in his pocket.

The frog spoke up again and said, 'If you kiss me and turn me back into a beautiful princess, I will stay with you for one week.'

The boy took the frog out of his pocket, smiled at it and returned it to his pocket. The frog then cried out, 'If you kiss me and turn me back into a princess, I'll stay with you and do ANYTHING you want!'

Again the boy took the frog out, smiled at it and put it back into his pocket. Finally, the frog asked, 'What is the matter? I've told you I'm a beautiful princess, that I'll stay with you for a week and do anything you want. Why won't you kiss me?'

The boy said, 'Look, I'm an accountant. I don't have time for a girlfriend but a talking frog is cool.'

A little old lady walked into the main branch of a New York bank holding a large paper bag in her hand. She told the young man at the window that she wished to take the $3 million that she had in the bag and open an account with the bank. But first she said that she wished to meet the president of the bank, owing to the large amount of money involved. After looking into the bag and seeing bundles of $1000 bills which could have amounted to $3 million, he called the president's office and saw to it that the old lady met with him. The lady was escorted upstairs and ushered into the president's office. Introductions were made and she explained that she liked to know the people that she did business with on a more personal level. The president then asked her how she came into such a large amount of money.

'Was it inheritance?' he asked.

'No,' she replied. He was quiet for a minute trying to think where she could have come into $3 million.

'I bet,' she stated.

'You bet!' repeated the president. 'As in horses?'

'No,' she replied. 'I bet on people.' Seeing his confusion, she explained that she just bet different things with people. All of a sudden she said, 'I'll bet you $25,000 that by 10 a.m. tomorrow your balls will be square.'

The bank president figured that she must be off her trolley and decided to take her up on the bet. He didn't see how he could lose. For the rest of the day he was very careful. He decided to stay home that evening and take no chances – there was $25,000 at stake. When he got up in the morning and took his shower, he checked to make sure that everything was OK. There was no difference, he looked the same as he always had. He went to work and waited for the little old lady to come in at 10 a.m., humming as he went. He knew that this would be a good day. How often do you get handed $25,000 for doing nothing? At 10 a.m. sharp, the little old lady was escorted into his office. With her was a younger man. When the president inquired as to the purpose of his being there, she informed him that he was her lawyer and that she always took him along when there was a large amount of money involved.

'Well,' she asked, 'how about our bet?'

'I don't know how to tell you this,' he replied, 'but I'm the same as I always have been, only $25,000 richer!' The lady seemed to accept this but requested that she be able to see for herself. The president thought that this was reasonable and dropped his trousers. She instructed him to bend over, then she grabbed hold of him. Sure enough everything was fine. The president then looked up and saw the lawyer banging his head against the wall.

'What's the matter with him?' the president asked.

'Oh him,' she replied. 'I bet him $100,000 that by 11 a.m. this morning I would have the president of the bank by the balls.'

Queen Victoria and the music hall artiste, Marie Lloyd, die and go before St Peter to find out if they'll be admitted to Heaven. Unfortunately, there's only one space left that day, so St Peter must decide which of them gets in. St Peter asks Marie if there's some particular reason why she should go to Heaven, so she takes off her top and says, 'Look at these. They're the most perfect ones God ever created and I'm sure it will please him to be able to see them every day for eternity.'

St Peter thanks her and asks Queen Victoria the same question. Queen Victoria drops her skirt and panties, takes a bottle of soda water out of her bag, shakes it up and douches with it.

St Peter says, 'OK, Victoria, you may go in. Have a nice day.'

Marie is outraged. She screams, 'What was that all about? I show you two of God's own creations, she performs a disgusting, pornographic act, and she gets in and I don't?!!'

'Sorry, Marie, but a royal flush beats a pair any day.'

There is a man who has three girlfriends but he does not know which one to marry. So he decides to give each one £5000 and see how they spend it.

The first one goes out and gets a total makeover with the money. She gets new clothes, a new hairdo, manicure, pedicure, the works, and tells the man, 'I spent the money so I could look pretty for you because I love you so much.' The second one went out and bought new golf clubs, a CD player, a television and a stereo, and gives them to the man. She says, 'I bought these gifts for you with the money because I love you so much.'

The third one takes the £5000 and invests it in the stock market, doubles her investment, returns the £5000 to the man and reinvests the rest. She says, 'I am investing the rest of the money for our future because I love you so much.' The man thought long and hard about how each of the women spent the money and decided to marry the one with the biggest tits.

A couple aged 67 went to the doctor's office. The doctor asked, 'What can I do for you?'

The man said, 'Will you watch us having intercourse?'

The doctor looked puzzled but agreed. When the couple had finished, the doctor said, 'There's nothing wrong with the way you have intercourse,' and charged them £32. This happened several weeks in a row. The couple would make an appointment, have intercourse, pay the doctor and leave.

Finally, the doctor asked, 'Just exactly what are you trying to find out?'

The old man said, 'Nothing. She's married and we can't go to her house. I'm married and we can't go to my house. The Holiday Inn charges £78. We do it here for £32 and I get £28 back from BUPA for a visit to the doctor's office.'

A husband and wife are on a nudist beach when suddenly a wasp buzzes into the wife's vagina. Naturally enough she panics. The husband too is quite shaken but manages to put a coat on her, pulls his shorts on, and carries her to the car. Then he makes a mad dash to the doctor.

The doctor, after examining her, says that the wasp is too far in to remove with forceps so he says to the husband that he will have to take it out by placing honey on his dick and withdrawing as soon as he feels the wasp on it. And so the honey is smeared, but because of his wife's screaming and his frantic rush to the doctor, and the panic, he just can't rise to the occasion.

So the doctor says he'll perform the deed if the husband and wife don't object. Naturally they agree for fear the wasp does any damage, and so the doctor quickly undresses, smears the honey on and instantly gets an erection, at which time he begins to fuck the wife. Only he doesn't stop and withdraw but continues with vigour.

The husband shouts, 'What the fuck is happening?' To which the doctor replies, 'Change of plan. I'm going to drown the fucker.'

Two aliens land in the middle of the Australian outback near a recently abandoned petrol station. The first alien goes up to the petrol pump (which he assumes to be an earthling) and says, 'Take me to your leader.'

The petrol pump doesn't say anything (naturally). The alien gets annoyed and demands again, 'Take me to your leader.'

When the petrol pump still doesn't reply, the alien gets mad and tells the petrol pump that if he doesn't start talking he will blast him.

At this point the second alien nervously interrupts, 'Er, sir, I don't think you should. . .' but the first alien will not be deterred and he blasts away.

There is a huge explosion and after the smoke clears the blackened aliens discover themselves lying 50 yards away from their destroyed space ship.

'You see, sir,' said the second alien, 'I didn't think it would be wise to mess with a guy who can wrap his dick around his waist and stick it in his ear.'

Two old ladies were waiting for a bus and one was smoking a cigarette. It started to rain so the old lady reached into her purse, took out a condom, cut off the tip and slipped it over her cigarette and continued to smoke. Her friend saw this and said, 'Hey, that's a good idea! What is it that you put over your cigarette?'

The other old lady said, 'It's a condom.'

'A condom? Where do you get those?'

The lady with the cigarette told her friend that you could purchase condoms at the pharmacy. When the two old ladies arrived downtown, the old lady with all the questions went into the pharmacy and asked the pharmacist if he sold condoms. The pharmacist said yes but looked a little surprised that this old woman was interested in condoms, so he asked her, 'What size do you want?' The old lady thought for a minute and said, 'One that will fit a Camel!'

Three couples new to the local area are looking to join a church parish. The vicar sets a pre-condition that each couple abstain from making love for two weeks, and sends them away.

On the follow-up interview, the vicar asked the older couple if they have managed to remain celibate. The couple had succeeded and were welcomed into the church. The second couple had also abstained and were welcomed aboard. On interviewing the youngest couple, the newly-weds, the husband confessed that their attempts had been in vain. On the thirteenth day his wife had reached up to grab a can of peas from a shelf and had dropped it. As she bent over to retrieve the can and showed her class, he had been overcome with lust and proceeded to give her a good seeing to on the spot.

The vicar commented, 'Well, I am afraid then, my children, that I cannot welcome you into the church.'

The husband replied, 'I understand father; to be honest with you we're not very welcome in Sainsbury's anymore either.'

◈

What's the square root of 69?

Ate something.

A woman decides that she's had it with trying to find a decent man in a bar. So, she takes out an ad in the paper that says she is seeking a mate who is loyal, rich and a good lover. After a few days, her doorbell rings. She opens the door and sees a man in a wheelchair with no arms and no legs.

He says, 'I'm here about your ad.'

Momentarily taken aback, she says, 'Well, how do I know you're loyal?'

'Well, I saved my platoon from the V.C. in 'Nam. That's where I lost my arms and legs,' he replies.

'How do I know you're rich?' she asks.

'I have my own software company and make $3 million a year. You can look at my bank statements,' he replies.

Looking at him in his wheelchair she demands, 'Well, how do I know that you're a good lover?'

He shrugs. 'I rang the doorbell, didn't I?'

On reaching his plane seat a man is surprised to see a parrot strapped in next to him. He asks the stewardess for a coffee, whereupon the parrot squawks, 'And get me a whisky, you cow.'

The stewardess, flustered, brings back a whisky for the parrot and forgets the coffee. When this omission is pointed out to her the parrot drains its glass and bawls, 'And get me another whisky you bitch.'

Quite upset, the girl comes back shaking with another whisky but still no coffee. Unaccustomed to such slackness the man tries the parrot's approach.

'I've asked you twice for a coffee, now go and get it or I'll give you a slap.'

Next moment both he and the parrot have been wrenched up and thrown out of the emergency exit by two burly stewards. Plunging downwards the parrot turns to him and says, 'For someone who can't fly you're a lippy bastard.'

Three dogs were in the vet's waiting room: a pit bull, a German shepherd and a Great Dane. The pit bull told the others, 'I was eating my dinner and my owner's two-year-old niece tried to grab my food so I bit her. Now they are going to put me to sleep.'

The German shepherd said, 'I chewed my master's shoes yesterday and now they are going to put me to sleep too.'

The Great Dane said, 'My master is a beautiful twenty-year-old woman. The other day she came out of the shower and bent over in front of me to pick up a towel, so I mounted her and did my thing.'

'So are you in here to be put to sleep too?' asked the others.

'No, I'm here to have my nails clipped!'

A little old lady sits at the lunch counter and orders a hamburger. The huge guy behind the counter bellows, 'One burger!'

The cook, who's even bigger, screams, 'Bur-ger!' whereupon he grabs a huge hunk of chopped meat, stuffs it under his bare armpit, pumps his arm a few times to squeeze it flat and then tosses it on the grill.

The old lady says, 'That's the most disgusting thing I think I've ever seen.'

The counterman says, 'Yeah? You should be here in the morning when he makes the doughnuts.'

A missionary gets sent into deepest darkest Africa and goes to live with a tribe therein. He spends years with the people, teaching them to read, write and the good Christian ways of the white man. One thing he particularly stresses is the evils of sexual sin. Thou must not commit adultery or fornication!

One day the wife of one of the tribe's noblemen gives birth to a white child. The village is shocked and the chief is sent by his people to talk with the missionary.

'You have taught us of the evils of sexual sin. One of our women has given birth to a white child and you are the only white man who has set foot in our village. It doesn't take a genius to work out what has been going on!'

The missionary replies, 'No, no, my good man. You are mistaken. What you have here is a natural occurrence – what is called an albino. Look to thy yonder field. Among that flock of white sheep is one black one. Nature does this on occasion.'

The chief pauses for a moment then says, 'Tell you what, you don't say anything about the sheep and I won't say anything about the child!'

One night a man heard howls coming from his basement and went down to discover a female cat being raped by a mouse. Fascinated by what he saw, the man gained the mouse's confidence with some cheese and then took him next door. The mouse repeated his amazing performance by raping a German shepherd. The man was very excited by this and was dying to show someone his discovery. The man rushed home and woke his wife up but before he could explain, she saw the mouse, screamed and covered her head with the blanket.

'Don't be afraid, darling,' said the man. 'Wait until I tell you about it.'

'Get out of here,' cried his wife, 'and take that sex maniac with you.'

A married woman is having an affair. Whenever her lover comes over, she puts her nine-year-old son in the closet. One day the woman hears a car in the driveway and puts her lover in the closet as well.

Inside the closet the little boy says, 'It's dark in here, isn't it?'

'Yes, it is,' the man replies.

'You wanna buy a baseball?' the little boy asks.

'No thanks,' the man replies.

'I think you do want to buy a baseball,' the little extortionist continues.

'OK. How much?' the man replies after considering the position he is in.

'Twenty-five dollars,' the little boy replies.

'TWENTY-FIVE DOLLARS!' the man repeats incredulously, but complies to keep him quiet.

The following week, the lover is visiting the woman again when she hears a car in the driveway and, again, places her lover in the closet with her little boy.

'It's dark in here, isn't it?' the boy starts off.

'Yes, it is,' replies the man.

'Wanna buy a baseball glove?' the little boy asks.

'OK. How much?' the hiding lover responds, acknowledging his disadvantage.

'Fifty dollars,' the boy replies and the transaction is completed.

The next weekend, the little boy's father says, 'Hey, son. Go get your ball and glove and we'll play some catch.'

'I can't. I sold them,' replies the little boy.

'How much did you get for them?' asks the father, expecting to hear the profit in terms of lizards and candy.

'Seventy-five dollars,' the little boy says.

'SEVENTY-FIVE DOLLARS! That's thievery! I'm taking you to the church right now. You must confess your sin and ask for forgiveness,' the father explains as he hauls the child away.

At the church, the little boy goes into the confessional, draws the curtain, sits down and says, 'It's dark in here, isn't it?'

'Don't you start that shit in here,' the priest says.

As an older couple were walking through the park, the woman noticed her partner eyeballing a younger female jogger's breasts as she was passing them, bralessly bouncing about in a tight T-shirt.

Once they had walked back home, the woman, craving such attention from her partner, removed her bra and put on a revealing T-shirt. Then she walks up to her partner holding up her arms and, turning a few times to show off her attributes, she says, 'Don't you think I look younger?'

The man is completely amazed at the sight before him and replies 'Why, yes my dear. All the wrinkles from your face have vanished . . .'

When the family learned that gramps was set to marry a twenty-year-old they were horrified. The eldest son took him aside and said, 'Frankly, Dad, we're concerned that sex with a young girl could prove fatal.'

'So what,' says the old codger. 'If she dies, she dies.'

They struck up a romance at the twilight Retirement Home and he put the hard word on her. They were quickly in his room where they started to undress.

'By the way,' she said as she flung off her blouse, 'I have acute angina.'

'Well, I hope it's better than those tits,' he replied.

Bill Gates dies in a car accident. He finds him-self being sized up by God.

'Well, Bill, I'm really confused on this call. I'm not sure whether to send you to Heaven or Hell. After all, you enormously helped society by putting a computer in almost every home in America, yet you also created that ghastly Windows '95. I'm going to do something I've never done before. I'm going to let you decide where you want to go.'

Bill replied, 'What's the difference between the two?'

God said, 'I'm willing to let you visit both places briefly, if it will help your decision.'

'Fine, but where should I go first?'

'I'll leave that up to you.'

'Okay then,' said Bill, 'let's try Hell first.'

So Bill went to Hell. It was a beautiful, clean, sandy beach with clear waters and lots of beautiful women running around, playing in the water, laugh-ing and frolicking about. The sun was shining; the temperature perfect. He was very pleased.

'This is great!' he told God. 'If this is Hell, I REALLY want to see Heaven!'

'Fine,' said God and off they went.

Heaven was a place high in the clouds with angels

drifting about, playing harps and singing. It was nice but not as enticing as Hell. Bill thought for a minute and made his decision.

'I think I'd prefer Hell,' he told God.

'Fine,' said God. 'As you desire.'

So Bill Gates went to Hell. Two weeks later, God decided to check on the late billionaire to see how he was doing there. When he got there, he found Bill shackled to a wall, screaming amongst hot flames in dark caves, being burned and tortured by demons.

'How's everything going?' he asked Bill.

Bill responded with his voice filled with anguish and disappointment. 'This is awful! This is nothing like the Hell I visited two weeks ago! I can't believe this is happening! What happened to that other place with the beaches and the beautiful women playing in the water?'

'That was the demo,' replied God.

A teenager comes home from school with a writing assignment. He asks his father for help.

'Dad, can you tell me the difference between potential and reality?'

His father looks up thoughtfully and says, 'I'll show you. Go and ask your mother if she would sleep with Robert Redford for a million dollars. Then go ask your sister if she would sleep with Brad Pitt for a million dollars. Then come back and tell me what you've learned.'

The kid is puzzled but he decides to see if he can figure out what his father means. He asks his mother, 'Mum, if someone gave you a million dollars, would you sleep with Robert Redford?'

His mother looks around slyly and then with a little smile says, 'Don't tell your father, but yes, I would.'

Then he goes to his sister's room and asks her, 'Sis, if someone gave you a million dollars, would you sleep with Brad Pitt?' His sister looks up and says, 'God! Definitely!'

The kid goes back to his father and says, 'Dad, I think I've figured it out. Potentially, we are sitting on two million bucks, but in reality, we are living with a couple of whores.'

An American, an Arab and a Mormon were having a couple of drinks in a bar and talking about their lives.

The American says, 'I have five kids and my wife is pregnant, so I will soon have a basketball team!'

The Arab replies, 'That's not bad, but I have ten kids and my wife is pregnant again, so I will then have a football team!'

Of course, the Mormon also wants to contribute to the conversation: 'So what? I have seventeen wives; one more and I will have a golf course!'

There's a drunk at one end of the bar and a woman in a tight low-cut dress at the other. The woman has her hand raised waving for the bartender, revealing an incredibly hairy armpit.

The drunk yells out, 'Give me a drink and give one to that ballerina down there.'

The bartender says, 'How do you know she's a ballerina?'

The drunk says, 'Who else could get her leg that high?'

A woman has been married for ten years and her husband always insisted on making love in the dark. One night, she grew tired of this, turned on the light and saw he was using a dildo on her.

'Honey, how could you do this? Explain yourself!' she wailed.

The husband replied, 'OK, I'll explain – but first you have to explain the kids.'

Why didn't Mexico field
a team for the summer
Olympics this year?

Because anyone who could run,
jump, or swim
was already in the USA.

Little Johnnie and his father are walking together when the boy asks his father a question.

'Dad, does Mum eat birds?'

'No, of course not,' says the father. 'Why?'

'Because the other day when I was walking past your bedroom door you asked her, "You wanna swallow or should I let it fly?"'

What's another definition
of dancing close together?

*A navel encounter without
the loss of semen.*

The eskimo's ski bike breaks down and he takes it to the garage to be fixed.

The mechanic says, 'I'll take a look at it for you.'

The eskimo decides to go for a spot of lunch and returns about an hour later.

The mechanic says, 'It looks like you've blown a seal, mate.'

'No,' says the eskimo. 'It's just a bit of mayonnaise.'

A captain in the foreign legion was transferred to a desert outpost. On his orientation tour he noticed a very old, seedy-looking camel tied up at the back of the enlisted men's barracks. He asked the sergeant giving the tour what the camel was for.

'Well, sir, it's a long way from anywhere and the men have natural sexual urges, so when they do, uh, we have the camel.'

The captain said, 'Well, if it's good for morale then I guess it's all right with me.'

After he had been at the fort for about six months the captain couldn't stand any more, so he told his sergeant to bring him the camel. The sergeant shrugged his shoulders and led the camel to the captain's quarters. The captain got on a footstool and proceeded to have vigorous sex with it. Satisfied, he stepped down from the stool and, buttoning up his trousers, asked the sergeant, 'Well, is that how the enlisted men do it?'

The sergeant replied, 'Well, sir, they usually just use it to ride to the brothel.'

Prince Charles is driving through the estate, when all of a sudden he hits something in the car. He jumps out, sees a corgi flat as a pancake. Shit, he thinks; what is Mother going to say? Out of the blue a genie appears and grants him a wish.

'Marvellous,' says Charles. 'Any chance of reviving this corgi?'

The genie takes a look and replies, 'My powers are limited. I could bring it back but it won't look too good. Is there anything else you want?'

Charles ponders and then says, 'My girlfriend, Camilla Parker-Bowles, could you make her young and beautiful?'

The genie frowns and then replies, 'Well, let's have another look at that corgi.'

Three male roommates decide to take out three female roommates on dates and report back the next morning.

The first guy says his date was a teacher, and that she kept saying, 'You're going to do this over and over till you get it right.'

The second guy says his date was a bit better because she was a nurse, and she just said, 'Lay back and relax . . . this won't hurt a bit.'

The third guy says his date must have been the best because she was a stewardess, and she only said, 'Put this over your nose and mouth and breathe deeply.'

A grocery delivery boy is making his rounds. He knocks on a door which is opened by a beautiful woman wearing nothing but a see-through negligee. She is very shapely in all departments. The young boy's jaw drops when he sees this beauty. She says to him, 'Quick, get inside. I hear someone coming.' He steps into her house. She shuts the door. She then lets the negligee drop to the floor revealing all to the boy. He can't take his eyes off her.

She asks him, 'Young man, what do you think is my most outstanding feature?' He takes his time looking her up and down and finally says, 'It would have to be your ears.' Puzzled she says, 'My ears?' The boy grins and says, 'Well, earlier, when you heard someone coming, that was me!'

Two builders, Fred and Bill, are seated either side of a table in a rough pub when a well-dressed man enters, orders a beer and sits on a stool at the bar. The two builders start to speculate about the occupation of the 'suit'.

FRED: I reckon he's an accountant.
BILL: No way . . . he's a stockbroker.
FRED: He ain't a stockbroker! A stockbroker wouldn't come in here.

The argument goes on for some time until the volume of beer gets the better of Fred and he makes for the toilet. On entering he sees that the 'suit' is standing at an urinal. Curiosity and several pints get the better of the builder.

FRED: 'Scuse me . . . no offence meant but me and my mate were wondering what you do for a living.
SUIT: No offence taken. I'm a Logical Scientist by profession.
FRED: Oh! What's that then?

SUIT: I'll try to explain by example. Do you have a goldfish at home?

FRED: Er . . . mm . . . well, yeah, I do as it happens.

SUIT: Well, it's logical to follow that you keep it in a bowl or a pond. Which is it?

FRED: It's a pond.

SUIT: Well then, it's reasonable to suppose that you have a large garden then?

FRED: Yes, I do have a big garden.

SUIT: Well then, it's logical to assume that, in this town, if you have a large garden you must have a large house?

FRED: As it happens, yes, I've got a five-bedroom house . . . built it myself.

SUIT: Well, given that you've got a five-bedroom house, it's logical to assume that you haven't built it for yourself and that you are probably married.

FRED: Yes, I am married. I live with my wife and three children.

SUIT: Well then, it's logical to assume that you are sexually active with your wife on a regular basis.

FRED: Yep! Four nights a week, me.

SUIT: Well then, it's logical to suggest that you do not masturbate very often.

FRED: Me? Never!

SUIT: Well, there you are! That's logical science at work. From finding out that you had a goldfish, I've told you about the size of your garden and house, your family and your sex life.

FRED: I see! That's pretty impressive ... thanks mate!

Both leave the toilet and Fred rejoins his mate.

BILL: I see the suit was in there. Did you ask him what he does?

FRED: Yep! He's a Logical Scientist.

BILL: What's that then?

FRED: I'll try and explain. Do you have a goldfish?

BILL: No.

FRED: Well then, Bill, you're a wanker!

A husband and wife love to play golf together but neither of them play very well so they decide to take private lessons. The husband has his lesson first. After the pro sees his swing he says, 'No, no, no! You're gripping the club way too hard.'

'Well, what should I do?' asks the man.

'Hold the club gently,' replied the pro, 'just like you'd hold your wife's breast.'

The man does this and makes a perfect swing, hitting the ball 250 yards straight up the fairway. He returns home and tells his wife the good news.

The next day the wife goes for her lesson. The pro watches her swing and says, 'No, no, no! You're gripping the club way too hard.'

'Well, what should I do?' she asks.

'Hold the club gently,' replied the pro, 'just like you'd hold your husband's penis.'

She does this and THUMP the ball goes straight down the fairway . . . about 15 feet.

'Well, that was nice and gentle,' says the pro, 'but now take the club out of your mouth and swing it like you're supposed to!'

A blonde goes into a worldwide message centre to send a message to her mother in Poland. When the man tells her the cost is $300 she exclaims, 'I don't have that kind of money but I'll do anything to get a message to my mother.'

'ANYTHING?' asks the man.

'Yes. Anything,' replies the blonde.

'Follow me,' says the man, walking into the next room and closing the door. He then says, 'Get on your knees,' and she does. He then says, 'Take down my zipper.' She does. 'Take it out,' he says and she does, holding it with both hands. The man then says, 'Well, go ahead!' She brings her head down and with her lips close to it says, 'HELLO MOM.'

What's the difference between a
lawyer and a prostitute?

*A prostitute stops screwing you
when you're dead.*

A Japanese tourist comes over for his honeymoon to England and at the bank he hands over a huge pile of yen. In return he gets a two-foot pile of pound coins. Overjoyed, he goes off and spends it on Barbour jackets, whiskey, cars and tours. But after a week he runs out of money so he does the same again. He hands over the same amount of yen but only gets a one-foot pile of pounds in return. He goes off and spends it on drink and food but runs out of money again. He returns to the bank and hands over the same amount of yen again but this time only gets a six-inch pile of pounds. This time he demands to see the manager.

'Why do I get a two-foot pile the first day, a one-foot pile the next and a six-inch pile today for the same amount of yen?' he asks.

'Fluctuations, sir. That's why,' replies the manager. To which the Japanese tourist replies, 'Fuck you Europeans too.'

Little Johnny is passing his parents' bedroom in the middle of the night on his way to get a glass of water. Hearing a lot of moaning and thumping, he peeks in and sees his folks jamming. Before his Dad has time to react, little Johnny says, 'Oh boy! Horsey ride! Can I ride your back, Dad?'

Dad, relieved that the kid doesn't realize what is going on, readily agrees and continues banging away. Pretty soon Mum starts moaning and gasping and little Johnny yells, 'Hang on tight, Dad. This is the part where me and the milkman usually get bucked off!'

Two engineering students meet on the campus one day. The first engineer calls out to the other, 'Hey, nice bike. Where did you get it?'

'Well,' says the second engineer, 'I was walking to class the other day when this pretty young co-ed rides up on this bike. She jumps off, takes off all her clothes and says, "You can have ANYTHING you want."'

'Good choice,' says the first. 'Her clothes wouldn't have fitted you anyway.'

A guy on a date parks his car and gets the girl in the back seat. They make love, but the girl wants it again and the guy complies. She wants more and they do it again. She still wants more, but this time the guy says he has to relieve himself.

While out of the car he notices a man half a block away changing a flat. He goes over to the man and says, 'Look, I've got this girl in my car and I've given it to her four or five times and she still wants more. I'll change your flat if you'll take over for me.'

The man agrees and he is just getting into the high numbers when a cop knocks on the window and shines a torch on them.

'What are you doing in there?' he asks.

The guy says, 'I'm making love to my wife.'

'Why don't you do that at home?' asks the cop.

The guy answers, 'To tell you the truth, I didn't know it was my wife until you shone the light on her.'

An Irishman walks into a bar in Dublin, orders three pints of Guinness and sits in the back of the room, drinking a sip out of each one in turn. When he finishes them, he comes back to the bar and orders three more. The bartender says to him, 'You know a pint goes flat after I draw it. It would taste better if you bought one at a time.'

The Irishman replies, 'Well, you see, I have two brothers. One is in America and the other is in Australia and I'm here in Dublin. When we all left home we promised that we'd drink this way to remember the days when we drank together.'

The bartender admits that this is a nice custom and leaves it at that. The Irishman becomes a regular in the bar and always drinks the same way, ordering three pints and drinking them in turn. One day he comes in and orders two pints. All the other regulars notice and fall silent. When he comes back to the bar for the second round the bartender says, 'I don't want to intrude on your grief but I wanted to offer my condolences on your great loss.'

The Irishman looks confused for a moment then a light dawns in his eye and he laughs.

'Oh no,' he says, 'everyone is fine. I've just quit drinking.'

Two missionaries in Africa get apprehended by a tribe of hostile cannibals who put them in a large pot of water, build a huge fire under it and leave them there. A few minutes later, one of the missionaries starts to laugh uncontrollably. The other missionary can't believe it. He says, 'What's wrong with you? We're being boiled alive! They're gonna eat us! What could possibly be funny at a time like this?'

The other missionary says, 'I just peed in the soup.'

'I haven't sold one tractor all month,' a tractor sales-man tells his friend.

'That's nothing compared to my problem,' his buddy replies. 'I was milking my cow when its tail whips around and hits me in the forehead, so I grabbed some string and tied its tail up to the rafters. Then I go back to milk it and it kicks me in the head with its right hind leg, so I grab some rope and tie the leg up to the rafters. I go back to try and milk it again and it kicks me in the head with its left hind leg, so I tie the leg up to the rafters. Then my wife comes walking in and I'll tell ya, if you can convince her that I was trying to milk that cow, I'll buy a tractor off ya.'

The teacher has set the class an assignment. He stresses the importance of the particular assignment and that no excuses will be accepted except illness (with a medical certificate) or a death in the immediate family.

A smart-arse student pipes up, 'What about extreme sexual exhaustion, sir?' The class breaks up laughing and when they settle down the teacher responds with, 'Well, Jones, I guess you'll have to learn to write with your other hand.'

There was a guy sitting at a bar having a beer. Up walks a so-called 'lady of the night'. She says, 'For three hundred dollars, I'll do anything you want.'

Our fine lad thinks for a moment, then says, 'Okay, paint my house.'

A girl goes into the doctor's office for a check-up. As she takes off her blouse he notices a red 'H' on her chest.

'How did you get that mark on your chest?' asks the doctor.

'Oh, my boyfriend went to Harvard and he's so proud of it that he never takes off his Harvard sweatshirt, even when we make love,' she replies.

A couple of days later another girl comes in for a check-up. As she takes off her blouse he notices a blue 'Y' on her chest.

'How did you get that mark on your chest?' asks the doctor.

'Oh, my boyfriend went to Yale and he's so proud of it that he never takes off his Yale sweatshirt, even when we make love,' she replies.

A couple of days later another girl comes in for a check-up. As she takes off her blouse he notices a green 'M' on her chest.

'Do you have a boyfriend at Michigan?' asks the doctor.

'No, but I have a girlfriend at Wisconsin. Why do you ask?'

In France, the young assistant pastors do not live in the main rectory. That is reserved for the pastor and his housekeeper. One day the pastor invited his new young assistant pastor to have dinner at the rectory. While being served, the young assistant pastor noticed how young, shapely and lovely the housekeeper was and deep down in his heart he wondered if there was more between the pastor and the housekeeper.

After the meal was over the middle-aged pastor assured the young priest that everything was purely professional . . . that she was the housekeeper and cook and that was that.

About a week later the housekeeper came to the pastor and said, 'Father, ever since the new assistant came for dinner I have not been able to find the beautiful silver gravy ladle. You don't suppose he took it, do you?'

The pastor said, 'Well, I doubt it but I'll write him a letter.' So he sat down and wrote:

Dear Father, I'm not saying you did take the gravy ladle. But the fact remains that it has been missing since you were here for dinner.

The young assistant received the letter and answered as follows:

Dear Father Pastor, I'm not saying that you do sleep with the housekeeper and I'm not saying that you do not sleep with the housekeeper. But I do know for sure that if you slept in your own bed you would find the gravy ladle.

Two baby whales are swimming in the sea, a boy and a girl, when they see a whaling ship.

'Hey, that's the ship that killed Dad. Let's get our revenge. If we take a really big gulp of air, swim down under the ship and blow it out through our blow holes, we can sink the ship.'

So the two young whales do exactly that: the ship rises soft into the air on a water spout, breaks up and sinks. When the water calms, hundreds of sailors are clinging to bits of wreckage and bobbing about in life vests.

'You know, it wasn't the ship that killed Dad, it was the sailors,' says the boy whale. 'To really get our revenge we should eat all the survivors.'

'No way,' says the girl whale. 'I agreed to do a blow-job but there's no way I'm going to swallow seamen!'

An old woman came into her doctor's office and confessed to an embarrassing problem. 'I fart all the time, Doctor, but they're soundless and they have no odour. In fact, since I've been here, I've farted no less than twenty times. What can I do?'

'Here's a prescription, Ms Smith. Take these pills three times a day for seven days and come back and see me in a week.'

Next week an upset Ms Smith marched into the doctor's office.

'Doctor, I don't know what was in those pills but the problem is worse! I'm farting just as much but now they smell terrible! What do you have to say for yourself?'

'Calm down, Ms Smith,' said the doctor soothingly. 'Now that we've fixed your sinuses, we'll work on your hearing.'

A preacher once had a pet parrot. He took him to church every Sunday and the bird would help lead choir practice. The parrot was a model pet most of the time but he had some serious problems on the side. You see, he liked to fuck chickens. The preacher kept telling him to stop it or he would shave the bird's head. Well, the parrot didn't listen and after several warnings the preacher got out the clippers and shaved the bird's head slicker than a peeled onion.

That Sunday in church, it was business as usual. The preacher was dividing the church members up for choir practice.

'All you ladies, come over here,' said the preacher, 'and all you gentlemen, please stand over there.'

About this time, a bald man walked by in front of the bird, to which the parrot said, 'And all you chicken fuckers over here beside me!'

There were three men who got lost in the forest and were captured by cannibals. The cannibal king then told the prisoners that they could live if they passed the trial. The first step of the trial was to collect ten fruits of the same kind. All three prisoners went their separate ways to gather fruit. The first one came back and said to the King, 'I have brought ten apples.'

The King then explained the trial to him. He was to shove the fruits up his arse without any noise or expression on his face or he would be eaten. The first apple went in but the second one made him wince in pain. He was eaten and he went to Heaven.

The second prisoner came back with ten berries and when the King explained the trial to him he thought to himself, This should be easy. 1 ... 2 ... 3 ... 4 ... 5 ... 6 ... 7 ... 8 ... On the ninth berry he burst out laughing and was also eaten.

The two prisoners met up in Heaven and the first one asked, 'Why did you laugh? You almost got away with it.'

The second one replied, 'I couldn't help it. I saw the third guy coming back with watermelons.'

Shortly after Christmas, the teacher of a grade-school class announced that if they wanted to, each child would be given the opportunity to tell about ONE special gift they had received. The first little girl stood and said, 'I got a bow-wow from my Daddy.'

The teacher addressed the class and sternly told them that they were certainly old enough to know and use the correct names for things and that she did not want to hear any more baby talk. She then asked the little girl if she could think of another word for her gift, one that grown ups would use.

The little girl replied, 'I got a puppy dog from my Daddy.'

The teacher praised her lavishly and went on to the next child, a boy.

'I got a choo-choo for Christmas,' he said.

Again the teacher chided the little boy and asked him to think of another name to describe his gift.

'I got an electric train,' he answered after mulling it over.

The teacher praised him for his effort. The next little boy, a normally very quiet kid, stood up and said, 'I got a book,' and sat down. Seeing an opportunity to draw him out a little, the teacher asked him what the title of his book was. The little boy hesitated and then with a serious face and knitted brow began did some deep thinking. After a couple of minutes his face brightened and he replied, 'Winnie the Shit.'

Little Red Riding Hood is on her way to Grandma's. Before she goes, her Mum says, 'Little Red Riding Hood, you'd better be careful because if the big bad wolf sees you he's going to hike up your little red dress, pull down your little red panties and fuck your little socks off.'

Red says, 'Don't worry, I've got a machete!'

On her way through the forest she bumps into the woodman who asks her where she is going.

'You'd better be careful. If the wolf sees you he'll hike up your little red dress, pull down your little red panties and fuck your little socks off,' he tells her.

'Don't worry, I've got a machete!' says Red.

Sure enough she arrives at her Grandma's and sees the big bad wolf sneaking up on her. He says, 'Come here little Red Riding Hood. I'm going to hike up your little red dress, pull down your little red panties and fuck your little socks off.'

Red pulls out her machete and says, 'No you're not! You're going to get down on your knees and eat me like the story says!!'

Who is the most popular guy at
the nudist colony?

*The guy who can carry two coffees
and a dozen doughnuts.*

Who is the most popular girl at
the nudist colony?

*The girl who can eat the
last doughnut.*

One Sunday morning William burst into the living room and said, 'Dad! Mom! I have some great news for you. I'm getting married to the most beautiful girl in town. She lives a block away and her name is Susan.'

After dinner, William's dad took him aside and said, 'Son, I have to talk to you. Your mother and I have been married thirty years. She's a wonderful wife but she has never offered much excitement in the bedroom, so I used to fool around with women a lot. Susan is actually your half-sister and I'm afraid you can't marry her.'

William was heartbroken. After eight months he eventually started dating girls again. A year later he came home and very proudly announced, 'Dianne said yes and we're getting married in June.'

Again his father insisted on another private conversation and broke the sad news. 'Dianne is your half-sister too, William. I'm very sorry about this.'

William was furious. He finally decided to go to his mother with the news.

'Dad's done so much harm. I guess I'm never going to get married,' he complained. 'Every time I fall in love, Dad tells me the girl is my half-sister.'

His mother just shook her head. 'Don't pay any attention to what he says, dear. He's not really your father.'

A ventriloquist walks into town and sees Dan sitting near his pad.

VENTRILOQUIST:	Hey, cool dog. Mind if I speak to him?
DAN:	Dog don't talk.
VENTRILOQUIST:	Hey dog, how's it going?
DOG:	Doin' alright.
DAN:	(extreme look of shock)
VENTRILOQUIST:	Is this your owner? (pointing at Dan)
DOG:	Yep.
VENTRILOQUIST:	How's he treat you?
DOG:	Real good. He walks me twice a day, feeds me great food and takes me to the lake once a week to play.
DAN:	(look of disbelief)
VENTRILOQUIST:	Mind if I talk to your horse?
DAN:	Horse don't talk.
VENTRILOQUIST:	Hey horse, how's it going?
HORSE:	Cool.
DAN:	(even more extreme look of shock)
VENTRILOQUIST:	Is this your owner?

	(pointing at Dan)
HORSE:	Yep.
VENTRILOQUIST:	How's he treat you?
HORSE:	Pretty good, thanks for asking. He rides me regularly, brushes me down often and keeps me in the barn to protect me from the elements.
DAN:	(total look of amazement)
VENTRILOQUIST:	Mind if I talk to your sheep?
DAN:	Sheep lie!

An eighteenth-century vagabond in England, exhausted and famished, came to a roadside inn with a sign reading George and the Dragon.

He knocked.

The innkeeper's wife stuck her head out of a window.

'Could ye spare some victuals?'

The woman glanced at his shabby, dirty clothes.

'No!' she shouted.

'Could I have a pint of ale?'

'No!' she shouted.

'Could I at least use your privvy?'

'No!' she shouted again.

The vagabond said, 'Might I please . . .'

'What now?' the woman screeched, not allowing him to finish.

'D'ye suppose,' he asked, 'that I might have a word with George?'

Three cowboys are sitting around a campfire out on the lonesome prairie, each with the bravado for which cowboys are famous. A night of tall tales begins.

The first says, 'I must be the meanest, toughest cowboy there is. Why just the other day a bull got loose in the corral and gored six men before I wrestled it to the ground by the horns with my bare hands.'

The second can't stand to be bested. 'Why, that's nothing. I was walking down the trail yesterday and a fifteen-foot rattler slid out from under a rock and made a move for me. I grabbed that snake with my bare hands, bit its head off and sucked the poison down in one gulp.

The third cowboy remained silent, slowly stirring the coals with his penis.

A man who smelled like a distillery flopped on a subway seat next to a priest. The man's tie was stained, his face was plastered with red lipstick and a half-empty bottle of gin was sticking out of his torn coat pocket. He opened his newspaper and began reading. After a few minutes the dishevelled guy turned to the priest and asked, 'Say, Father, what causes arthritis?'

'Mister, it's caused by loose living, being with cheap wicked women, too much alcohol and a contempt for your fellow man.'

'Well, I'll be damned,' the drunk muttered returning to his paper.

The priest, thinking about what he had said, nudged the man and apologized. 'I'm very sorry. I didn't mean to come on so strong. How long have you had arthritis?'

'I don't have it, Father. I was just reading here that the Pope does.'

A man who just got a raise decided to buy a new scope for his rifle. He goes to a rifle shop and asks the clerk to show him a scope. The clerk takes out a scope and says to the man, 'This scope is so good you can see my house all the way up on that hill.' The man takes a look through the scope and starts laughing.

'What's so funny?' asks the clerk.

'I can see a naked man and a naked woman running around the house,' replies the man.

The clerk grabs the scope from the man and looks at his house. Then he hands two bullets to the man and says, 'Here are two bullets. I'll give you this scope for nothing if you take these two bullets, shoot my wife's head off and shoot the guy's dick off.'

The man takes another look through the scope and says, 'You know what? I think I can do that with one shot!'

One day Johnny met the captain of the local cricket team who said to him, 'We're one man short on the team today. Can you open for us?'

'What do I get out of it?' asks Johnny.

The captain who is also a poultry farmer says, 'I'll give you one of my prime free range ducks.'

So Johnny pads up and stands at the crease waiting for the opening ball. It's a spinner and Johnny can't handle these too well and he's out. Johnny makes his way home after his less than glowing performance but he's happy with his duck. On the way he meets Agnes who asks him if he wants a bit. Johnny replies that he has no money.

'That's okay. I'll take the duck,' replies Agnes. Johnny thinks that this is a fair exchange and gives one of the best performances of his life which leaves Agnes panting for more.

'Will you do that again?' asks Agnes.

'But what do I get out of it?' he asks.

'I'll give you back this duck,' replies Agnes.

Once more, Johnny and Agnes retreat into carnal ecstasy. Later on, Johnny is walking home with a big smile on his face. Suddenly the duck slips from his grasp and falls under the wheels of a passing car. The car screeches to a halt and the captain of the cricket team gets out.

'I'm terribly sorry about the duck, Johnny. Look, here's fifteen pounds.'

Johnny takes the money and picks up the semblance of a duck from the road. He returns home with an even bigger smile on his face.

'What's the smile for, Johnny?' asks his Mum.

'Well,' he replies, 'I got a duck for a duck, a fuck for a duck, a duck for a fuck, fifteen quid for a fucked-up duck and I've still got the fucking duck!'

A young couple are out one night and while driving down the highway the guy says to the girl, 'If I go a hundred miles an hour, will you take your clothes off?'

She agrees and he begins to speed up. When the speedometer hits 100 she starts to strip. When she has taken all of her clothes off, the guy is so busy staring at her that he drives off the road and flips the car. The girl is thrown clear without a scratch, but her clothes and her boyfriend are trapped in the car.

'Go get help,' he pleads.

She replies, 'I can't, I'm naked.'

He points to his shoe that was thrown clear and says, 'Cover your snatch with that and go get help.'

She takes the shoe and covers herself and runs to the gas station down the road. When she arrives she is frantic and yells to the attendant, 'Help! Help! My boyfriend's stuck!'

The attendant looks down at the shoe covering her crotch and replies, 'I'm sorry, Miss. He's too far in.'

Stefan and his grandfather are fishing. Grandpa pulls out a beer and the little boy says, 'Grandpa, can I have some?' Grandpa says, 'Is your penis long enough to touch your asshole?' The little boy says, 'No.'

'Then you can't have any,' says Grandpa.

A while later, Grandpa pulls out a cigar and the boy says, 'Can I have one of those?' Grandpa says, 'Is your penis long enough to touch your asshole?' Again, the little boy says, 'No.'

'Then you can't have one,' says Grandpa.

After fishing they go to the grocery story for food and each buys a lottery ticket. Grandpa is unlucky but Stefan wins $50,000.

'Great! You're going to split that with me, aren't you son?'

The little boy says, 'Grandpa, is your penis long enough to touch your asshole?'

'Yes,' replies Grandpa.

'Then go fuck yourself.'